Stress Busting

Stress Busting

Michael Papworth

continuum
LONDON • NEW YORK

Continuum

The Tower Building
11 York Road
London SE1 7NX

15 East 26th Street
New York
NY 10010

www.continuumbooks.com

© Michael Papworth 2003

British Library Cataloguing-in-Publication Data
A catalogue record for this book is available from the British Library.

ISBN 0–8264–7069–6

Typeset by BookEns Ltd, Royston, Herts.
Printed and bound in Great Britain by Biddles Ltd, Guildford and King's Lynn

Contents

Contents

Series Introduction

Dear Teacher

Classmates is an exciting and innovative new series developed by Continuum, and is designed to help you improve your teaching, and your career.

With your huge workload both inside and outside of school, we understand that you have less and less time to read around your profession. These short, pithy guides have been designed with an accessible layout so that you don't have to wade through lots of dull, heavy text to find the information you need.

All our authors have experienced teaching first hand and have written this essential series with busy teachers in mind. Our subjects range from taking school trips (*Tips for Trips*) and dealing with parents (*Involving Parents*) to coping with the large amounts of stress in your life (*Stress Busting*) and creating more personal time for yourself (*Every Minute Counts*).

If you have practical advice that you would like to share with your fellow teachers and think you could write a book for this series then we would be delighted to hear from you.

We do hope you enjoy reading our *Classmates*.

With very best wishes,

Continuum's Education Team

P.S. Watch out for our second batch of ten *Classmates*, to be launched in March 2004.

Preface

Teaching is a stressful job, there is no getting away from it. Any job involving people, difficult goals and time-pressure is going to be stressful. There is nothing that can be done to completely remove the stress from teaching simply because teaching is about all the things that cause stress. Teaching is about young people, a significant minority of whom don't want to be there and who may cause a disproportionate amount of difficulty. Teaching is about helping as many of these young people as possible get a good education – and we have a decreasing resource base with which to do it. Teaching is about getting the job done, but the goal posts move with heartbreaking irregularity. No sooner do we get used to one system than it is changed and everything has to be reorganized.

Yes, of course, the stress can be reduced, but it can NEVER be completely eliminated. That does not mean that we should simply accept the situation as it is. But it does mean that we need to have a realistic view of life.

There is certainly very much that can be done to remove the unnecessary stress caused by excessive workload, paperwork, indiscipline and death-by-a-thousand-initiatives. The government, unions, LEAs and individual schools and their management teams are making great efforts to reduce the stress in teaching. They are having a degree of success, but it is a slow process.

We can't wait that long! This little book is my offering to help colleagues do what they can on a personal level.

It deals with five major topics followed by a section of quick tips:

About stress: A clear and concise explanation of the essential nature of stress and the physical and mental results of the stress reaction.

Reduce your stress with ARC: A simple (and that doesn't mean easy) approach to reducing the stress in your life.

Physical resilience: You have to be physically able to deal with life's stresses. This chapter explains the most basic essentials for good physical health and resilience.

Mental resilience: You have to be mentally able to deal with life's stresses. This chapter explains the most basic essentials for good mental health and resilience.

Emotional resilience: Together with those in the medical professions, emergency services, fighting forces and social support services we see many emotionally disturbing instances. We have to be resilient and not allow these to cloud our judgement.

Quick tips: There are many very simple steps that you can take which can reduce the level of stress that your job induces. This is a simple list gathering together the most generally applicable of them.

You will find it helpful to read this book with a pencil in your hand and a notebook handy. Highlight the parts of the book that you find particularly useful so you can find them again when you want to. Use the notebook to do the exercises scattered through the book and to make your own notes. The more that you interact with the book and become personally involved, the more you will benefit.

Enjoy.

Michael Papworth
Worcester

1

About Stress

- What is stress?
- Why do we get stressed?
- How does stress affect us?
- Acute stress and chronic stress
- What are the dangers of chronic stress?
- We are all suffering from chronic stress
- What are the symptoms of chronic stress?
- Ask the right question to get the right answer

What is stress?

There is much debate over what is an accurate definition of stress. I can almost guarantee that you won't find two experts in the field that will agree, but this is common among experts. This is about the simplest and most complete definition I have found:

Stress is the physical and mental reaction to a challenge.

Before we go any further, I should mention that there are two types of stress. They are called eustress and distress.

Stress Busting

- Eustress is the kind of stress that you want in your life. It is the buzz that you get when you are doing things that have a degree of challenge, but are enjoyable.

- Distress is the stress that we all talk about. This is the kind of stress that you feel when you are faced with a challenge that is either not of your own choosing or that you feel you cannot face. In this book I shall refer to stress meaning distress.

If you or I were to be faced with a murderous thug determined to beat us to death, we would feel distress. Mike Tyson, on the other hand, would feel eustress.

The idea of jumping out of a light aircraft with a bag of flimsy fabric strapped to my back causes me distress. Others, who do it regularly at weekends, find it exhilarating and full of eustress.

The implication is obvious: *Your stress reaction is idiosyncratic and depends entirely upon your perception of situations and events.*

This is a vitally important point and one to which I will be returning.

Why do we get stressed?

Imagine one of your distant male ancestors hunting on the plains of Africa. He is creeping through the long grass, spear in hand. He is sweeping his eyes from side to side trying to catch the tell-tale signs of prey or predator in his acute central vision. His peripheral vision reassures him that his fellow hunters

'Your stress reaction is idiosyncratic and depends entirely upon your perception of situations and events' are close by and will catch any slight movement indicating danger. He is relaxed and fully aware of everything going on around him.

Suddenly, he catches sight of a movement in the grass. He recognizes the movement and he catches the sweet scent of deer.

His body and brain are flooded with chemicals, his muscles tense, his eyes dilate and his nostrils flare.

Meanwhile, back at the encampment, his mate is tending the fire and shelling nuts while keeping an eye on the infants playing nearby. She is happily chatting to her sisters and cousins and calling to the babies. She is relaxed and fully aware of everything going on around her.

Suddenly, out of the corner of her eye, she catches sight of a flash of green and yellow between a couple of rocks. Just the other side of the rocks is a baby crawling after a beetle. In a moment or two the baby and snake will startle each other.

Her body and brain are flooded with chemicals, her muscles tense, her eyes dilate and her nostrils flare.

She picks up a stick and rushes to save the baby and kill the snake with no thought of anything else. The other women and the children scream in fear and dash to safety.

The hunter, the women and the children have all experienced a stress reaction. Their brains and bodies underwent dramatic and profound changes to enable them to cope with a challenge.

We get stressed because it is a survival mechanism (and it is common to all animals). If we were always in the same laid-back, relaxed and aware state of constant happiness and bliss, our species would have been killed off by the first sabre-toothed tiger that wandered into the cave.

How does stress affect us?

Your entire organism is affected by any kind of challenge. Both your brain and your body undergo changes designed to aid your survival. These changes occur rapidly and automatically.

Changes in the brain

Your brain is made up of four functional units. We are only concerned with three of them here. They are the:

1. *Brain stem*: the part of your brain that keeps you alive. It controls your vital functions and instincts. The brain stem is an extension of your spinal cord and is the conduit for all information to and from your lower body. It is the most primitive part of the brain and is often referred to as the reptilian brain.

2. *Limbic system*: the part of your brain that controls your emotions and parts of your memory, and acts like a control centre. All your sensory input is fed into the limbic system first and is either rejected or sent to other parts of the brain for processing. It grows on top of the brain stem and is made up of many different units. It is frequently called the mammalian brain.

3. *Cerebrum*: this is your thinking and learning brain and is what makes you human. It is huge in comparison to other mammals and is fully 85 per cent of your brain's mass.

5

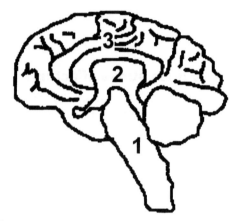

When you experience a challenging event, your limbic system shuts down your cerebrum and switches your brain stem into alert mode. You still have access to your lower cerebral functions (like speech) but you are quite simply unable to think. Your behaviour becomes 100 per cent animal.

[OK. For all you biology teachers, I know that this is an oversimplified explanation. But it's near enough!]

Changes in the body

When you are faced with a challenge, your brain and endocrine (hormone-producing) system flood your body with chemicals to prepare you to deal with life-and-death situations.

◆ Your large muscles tense and are flooded with adrenaline ready for massive exertion and super-strength.

6

- Your pupils dilate to take in more light and your nostrils flare to aid in rapid breathing.

- Your heart rate and blood pressure increases to supply more blood to essential organs and major muscles.

- Your blood thickens and is suffused with clotting chemicals ready to repair any damage to your skin or major organs.

- Blood is diverted from organs inessential to short-term survival.

- Bowels are loosened to rid the body of excess mass which would slow down flight or fight.

It really is a brilliantly designed system. Your whole organism is designed to react to challenges in order to keep you alive. You can either fight with incredibly enhanced strength and speed or run away fast and escape the danger.

What is more, all this happens in an instant. Immediately that sabre-toothed tiger enters the cave, you are ready for the fight or flight. (Freeze would not be a good choice in this particular instance.)

Of course, the process is the same in other, more modern, situations. When a small child runs into the street from between two cars right in front of you, it's your brain stem that slams on the brakes. If you see two dark-clad youths skulking near the entrance to an alley way at night, it's your brain stem that makes you clench your fists and quickens your pulse. When a child makes a completely unexpected violent reaction to a perfectly reasonable request pleasantly made, it's your brain stem that makes you want to throttle her.

Acute stress and chronic stress

Acute stress is when we face huge challenges on an irregular basis. This is exactly what we (and all other animals) are designed to withstand. We are stressed, we face the danger or flee, we survive or we are killed. End of story.

Chronic stress is when we are subjected to very frequent stress for extended periods.

Your reaction to high-level and low-level stress is the same. The only difference is one of degree.

In the acute stress situation, your entire organism is suffused with chemicals which are consumed and then you return to equilibrium. In the chronic stress situation, your body is constantly suffused with these chemicals.

What are the dangers of chronic stress?

Chronic stress has a negative effect on your on-the-job performance, your family, your social life, your sex life and your general outlook on life. It also has a dramatically negative effect on your mental and organic health.

Physical

Stress can cause a large number of muscular aches and pains as your body is under a constant tension.

Your posture, poise and general appearance suffer and this can lead to skeletal complaints.

Your circulatory system is adversely affected. Blood pressure is raised, your blood is thickened and your cholesterol level is raised. This can lead to cardio-vascular problems, heart disease, heart attack and stroke.

Your digestion is slowed down and peristalsis is either sped up or slowed down. It is now known that stress doesn't cause stomach ulcers directly, but that it is a contributory factor. Bowels can become loose and movements involuntary.

There is a growing body of evidence that stress can cause your immune system to become suppressed. This is thought to be a contributory factor in a whole host of problems from an inability to withstand colds to susceptibility to cancers.

Mental

Your whole composure and ability to think straight is affected by chronic stress. This is because your brain switches away from thinking mode to survival mode. Distressing thoughts can invade your head and be very difficult to overcome. Concentration and memory are severely impaired. Sleep problems can become the norm. Self-speak can become unhelpful and even destructive and your entire self-image distorted.

Family and social

Prolonged stress can have a very serious effect on your family and social life. It is not in the least bit

9

unusual to release built-up stress and attendant anger and frustration on unsuspecting family and friends. The sad fact is that no one finds it very easy to love a long-term grouch.

Job performance

Your ability to perform your job becomes severely compromised as your personal effectiveness diminishes. This can lead to either apathy (doing the very minimum or even less) or overwork (in an attempt to make up for loss of effectiveness). Classroom performance suffers and interpersonal relationships with kids and colleagues can become strained or even destructive.

To put it as simply as possible, if you are suffering from chronic stress, your entire organism and life is out of balance.

We are all suffering from chronic stress

We, in our modern society, are constantly under a level of stress. There is stress from noise, unsocial pupils, time pressure, constant changes in our environment and social pressure to deny our essential animal nature. The only question is to what extent are we suffering.

The three major causes of stress at work are:

- people
- change
- lack of control over the process

Doesn't that sound like teaching?

Selye's general adaptation syndrome (GAS) model

There are three stages in this model of the stress reaction.

Alarm: autonomic response to a stressor – flight, fight or freeze.

Resistance: a transient stage that generally shows resistance to stress symptoms and illnesses. Prolonged exposure to stressors produces the next stage.

Exhaustion: burnout, serious illness due to decreased ability to ward off physical and mental challenges.

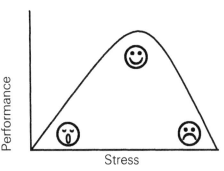

The performance-stress curve

The curve above shows how performance is affected by stress.

◆ The left-hand end of the curve shows that a stress-free life leads to boredom and low performance.

◆ The central portion shows that an acceptable level

of stress leads to peak performance. This is where you want to be.

◆ The right-hand end of the curve shows that excessive stress leads to lowered performance and eventual burnout.

You might naively imagine that the more effort that you put into your work, the better your performance will be. This curve shows that this is true, but only to an extent. Enough is enough. Too much is counter-productive and ultimately destructive.

What are the symptoms of chronic stress?

The table below shows some of the major symptoms that chronic stress frequently induces. It is by no means exhaustive.

Physical	Mental	Emotional
weight change	lack of concentration	frustration
insomnia	low productivity	anger
digestive upsets	lack of clarity	worry
nervous actions	staleness	joylessness
frequent minor ailments	negative self-speak	blame-laying

If you recognize a few of these in yourself, you are stressed beyond the acceptable limit. If you recognize more than a few, you should seek help immediately. There is absolutely no merit in denying the danger signals.

Your life should be joyful. You have a perfect right

to be joyful. Your family and friends and everybody else who knows you want you to be joyful. Joy is your primary duty. For if you are not joyful yourself, how are you going to spread joy in the world?

Ask the right question to get the right answer

The question is not, 'Are you stressed?'

The question is, 'How stressed are you?'

	not at all	slightly	quite	very	to the limit
Physically Mentally Emotionally					

The next question is, 'How far is this stress affecting your life?'

	not at all	slightly	quite a lot	very much	to the limit
Home Work Social Sex Self-image Relationships Efficacy					

The final question is, 'What are you going to do about it?' Take your notebook and start thinking about this straight away.

13

2

Reduce your Stress with ARC

- The meaning of ARC
- The 80–20 law
- How to avoid stressors
- How to reframe stressors
- How to cope with stressors

The meaning of ARC

The acronym ARC stands for

- Avoid
- Reframe
- Cope

and represents a hierarchy of approaches to eliminating much of the distress in your life.

The idea is very simple. You look at your life and analyse what the major stressors are. Stressors fall into two main categories. There are stressors due to external influences and those due to internal influences. You need to know what the stressors in your life are – you have to identify the enemy! You then re-design your life to avoid what you can. What you can't avoid, you reframe (change the way you perceive them). What you cannot avoid or reframe, you simply have to cope with.

The 80–20 law

This is a natural law discovered by an Italian economist by the name of Wilfredo Pareto and often bears the name 'The Pareto Principle'. It states that 80 per cent or more of the results you get flow from 20 per cent or less of the causes.

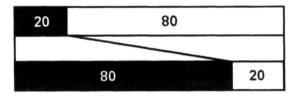

This is very non-intuitive. You might naively imagine that cause and effect are in direct proportion, but just a few moments of thought will show you that this is not, in fact, the case at all.

To understand the law consider a few examples:

- ◆ 80 per cent or more of speeding tickets are collected by 20 per cent or less of motorists

- ◆ 80 per cent or more of the trouble in your school is caused by 20 per cent or less of the kids

- ◆ 80 per cent or more of the wealth of any country is owned by 20 per cent or less of the population

You can now probably understand that 80 per

'You need to know what the stressors in your life are – you have to identify the enemy!'

cent or more of the distress in your life is caused by 20 per cent or less of the stressors.

The implication is obvious. If you can identify that 20 per cent and find a way of dealing with them (using ARC), you will reduce the stress by fully 80 per cent or more!

Just in case you are not convinced by this, think about another situation. You are driving a four by four along a narrow and little-used mountain road. As you round a bend you see that the road is blocked by a landslide. There are a few boulders, quite a lot of fairly large rocks and the greatest part of it is gravel.

What are you going to do?

You are going to get rid of the boulders first! They are the biggest obstacles. You will then get the bigger rocks out of the way and then you can just drive over the gravel.

That's pretty much the approach that you will use to make progress in life. You simply must clear the path. Get the biggest obstacles out of the way so that you can drive your way forward without worrying too much about a bit of gravel here and there.

By far the most important thing that you can do right now is to spend time looking at your life very honestly and seeing where your major stressors are. You'll need to take a bit of time to do this and keep that notebook handy.

Look at your life and give yourself a rating for the following:

Time: Do you have enough time for the important things in your life?

17

Stress Busting

Control: Do you have enough control over your life to give you comfort?

Environment: Are you comfortable with your physical environment?

Find the bigger problems and commit yourself to addressing them first. I promise you, if you can get the bigger problems dealt with, the remaining smaller ones will be much easier to handle.

How to avoid stressors

If you always do what you've always done, you'll always get what you've always got.
Consider the times that you feel most stressed. What are the external causes? Which of these can you simply avoid?

◆ If you find that your system for handling paper-work is inefficient and wastes your time, make a big effort to take control of the system and find one that works for you.

◆ If a particular child is always causing you confrontations and grief, find a way of defusing situations before they arise.

◆ If you are constantly in a rush at school and find that time is in control of you, re-assess the way that you use time and take control of it for yourself.

I am not trivializing this. I didn't say that this was going to be an easy ride. In fact I can guarantee that much of it WON'T be easy. If it was easy, you would have done it already.

You will need to make changes in the way that you do things. If you don't, you'll remain with the same problems.

Of course, there are going to be some major stressors that you simply cannot avoid. In this case, try reframing.

How to reframe stressors

If you always see what you've always seen, you'll always be where you've always been.

Consider the times that you feel most stressed. What are the internal causes?

Remember that you don't see things as they are: you see them as you are. The world takes on the colour of the lenses that you wear when you look at it. If your lenses are not perfect, your view of the world will be distorted.

Do you remember the point earlier about stress being an idiosyncratic reaction? That's because you are the designer of your own lenses!

You have to change your lenses.

Let me give you an example:

Some time ago I met a deputy head who was stressed to the limit and then some. The particular situation was that she had to deal with a boy who had committed a nasty assault on another pupil. The boy was denying it in the face of overwhelming evidence. This lady was at her wit's end trying to get through to this boy

19

and was becoming extremely upset and close to cracking up.

We talked for quite some time. Eventually she began to realize that it wasn't her problem. She was being perfectly decent, honest, upright and forthright. She had no problems at all. It was the boy who was being deceitful, dishonest and downright unpleasant. The problems lay entirely with him.

The situation was that she was getting angry and frustrated. Although she didn't fully appreciate it, this is a sign of weakness. The boy was thoroughly enjoying making someone (who was supposed to be in authority) feel weak and powerless.

She imagined that she was in control, but the reality was that she had ceded her control to a very immature boy. She was, in fact, being controlled. This boy, knowingly or otherwise, was controlling her level of frustration and anger by his behaviour.

Once she readjusted her lenses, she could immediately see the way forward. She returned to the fray.

Within a few minutes that boy emerged from her office in floods of tears willing to take the punishment handed out and determined to make full amends for his assault.

He also saw the situation through new lenses.

That is reframing.

As long as you are doing your very best and performing at the highest level, you have absolutely nothing to worry about.

- If a child wants a confrontation, it's not your problem. It's his or her problem. You have to help him or her deal with it.

- If a colleague is being unpleasant, it's not your problem. You have to help him or her realize that they are not adopting constructive strategies for getting what they really want. If you can't help them, don't lose sleep over it.

    In order to reframe, you need to ask yourself:

- Whose problem is it really?

- Who is out of balance with their reality?

- Who is behaving badly?

- Who is being destructive?

- Who is being weak?

Identify the REAL owner of the problem.

    If it really is your problem, deal with it. If it isn't your problem, there is no need to be stressed!

    Again, I am not trivializing this at all. You may well need to invest a great deal of time and effort in this. It isn't easy to change your lenses at will. If you have spent a considerable proportion of your life accepting responsibility for other people's problems, you cannot change this overnight.

    You may also need to learn new skills. If you are inclined towards being over-accommodating or to-wards bullying (both of which are stress-inducing) you will need to learn assertive behaviour.

21

How to cope with stressors

It goes without saying that even if you are able to avoid a great deal of the stress in your life, and no matter how much you are able to reframe, there is always going to be a residual amount. There's just no way round this, and you don't want to find a way round it. Remember the performance-stress curve. You need a certain amount of stress in your life in order to add a bit of zest.

In order to cope with stress you need to be resilient. You need to be resilient physically and mentally.

Teaching IS stressful. There is no way it could be otherwise. Any job which involves dealing with people, dealing with change and which allows very little in the way of autonomy is going to be stressful.

If you are to be a successful teacher and a happy human being you need this resilience.

That's what the next three sections are about.

Review

- Learn the acronym ARC: Avoid, Reframe, Cope. This is a hierarchy.

- Use the 80-20 law. Identify the major stressors in your life and deal with them first.

- Redesign your life to *Avoid* as much stress as possible.

- *Reframe* stressors by making sure that your lenses are clear and distortion-free.

- Make sure that you can *Cope* with life's stress by making yourself resilient.

3

Physical Resilience

♦ Introduction

♦ Breathing

♦ Weight and nutrition

♦ Exercise

♦ Rest

♦ Deep muscular relaxation

Introduction

Hominids not so very different to you and me have been walking this planet for somewhere between three and four million years. During most of that time they have lived in the wild, hunted and foraged for their food, lived in supportive family groups and died at a young age.

Our society has evolved very rapidly over the past few thousand years, but our basic biological needs are identical to those of our earliest ancestors. We now live a life which is about as far removed from our natural life as it is possible to get. Even the revolutions which are bound to occur in the future will have little additional impact on our distance from our natural environment.

Our bodies are regularly assaulted with an estimated 10,000 non-naturally occurring chemicals in the food we eat, the drinks we consume and the air we breathe as well as the everyday objects with which we come into contact. Our work is largely sedentary. Entertainment for most of us consists of sitting in front of a cathode ray tube or ingesting alcohol – sometimes both!

We abuse our bodies from the cradle to the grave. Children no longer play in the street but spend hours in front of computers or TVs. Most people drive everywhere. We spend nearly as many hours in front of the TV as we do at work and then eat chemically enhanced convenience foods because we don't have time to cook.

Nearly everyone in the Western world is so physically stressed that it's hard to know where to start.

Let's start at the beginning.

Breathing

We all breathe, and most of us do it wrongly.

In order to inspire air you need to create a partial vacuum in your chest cavity. This requires that you increase the volume of your chest cavity. In order to expire air, you have to do the reverse.

There are two ways of controlling this pressure variation.

The first and most common method is to expand

and contract the rib cage which causes the chest to rise and fall. This method is called Chest Breathing and is very ineffective.

The second method is to move the diaphragm into and out of the chest cavity. The rib cage doesn't move. This method is called Belly Breathing (because your belly moves in and out) and is the correct and natural way of breathing. Belly Breathing is much deeper breathing and is far more beneficial. If you need convincing of this, find yourself a sleeping baby and watch her carefully. You will unfailingly find that her little belly is moving in and out. Babies have the advantage of not having learned bad posture and poor breathing habits.

Don't underestimate the importance of your posture on breathing. Here's a little experiment you can try immediately, and you can do it either standing or sitting. Slouch forwards as much as you can so your shoulders are well forwards of your hips and your belly is squashed up. Take the deepest breath that you can and hold it. Now return to an upright well-balanced position and breathe in again.

Do you see how you can get much more air into your lungs when you are upright? The simple fact is that slouching reduces your breathing capacity. (It also does so for the kids in your classes. The very first rule in class should be 'Sit up straight.' Slouching reduces breathing efficiency and consequently reduces the activity of the brain because of oxygen deprivation.)

In order to practise Belly Breathing, sit comfortably but upright. Place one hand flat on the bottom of your rib cage over the sternum and the other hand flat just

25

over your belly button. When you breathe in you should feel your rib cage remain static and your belly expand. As you breathe out, you should feel your belly contract.

When you are standing, stand naturally and easily. Don't try to hold in your belly and stick your chest out. When you are sitting, sit upright with your shoulders above your hips. Never slouch whether sitting or standing.

Belly Breathing is very relaxing. Just a few rounds of deep Belly Breathing (which may only take 30 seconds or so) calms the mind and cools the temper and puts a whole new complexion on the day.

Weight and nutrition

There is a chance that you're not going to like this! You need:

♦ 1 large heavy-grade paper bag (NOT plastic)

♦ 1 full-length mirror

♦ Absolute privacy

Instructions:

1. Remove all your clothes.

2. Place the paper bag over your head.

3. Punch holes so you can see out of the paper bag.

4. Look at yourself in the mirror.

What do you see?

The question is not whether you look like Demi Moore or Bruce Willis with a paper bag over her/his head. The question is whether you look right. Do you look like you want to look?

Believe me, please. What you are looking at is what everybody else is looking at. OK, it's covered in clothes most of the time, but while clothes can enhance a good figure, they cannot hide a bad figure.

If you are round-shouldered without clothes, you are also round-shouldered with clothes and no one else thinks otherwise. If you are overweight and think that the clothes that you wear mask it, forget it! They don't.

Please, for your own benefit, face it. Everyone knows exactly what you look like.

And now so do you.

Of course, your weight doesn't only have a cosmetic dimension. There is also a very much more important health dimension.

There are three basic body types. They are called:

◆ Apple: given to storing fat around the waist.

◆ Pear: given to storing fat around the hips

◆ Greyhound: not generally given to storing fat.

The point is that ANY of these body types can look good as long as the body fat is under control. However, be aware that a slim apple (for example) is not a greyhound. The body type you have is the body type you have. If you don't like it, you should have chosen your parents with more care.

Of these three types, it is the apple who is in the

27

greatest need of weight control. This is because the apple-shaped don't only store fat subcutaneously; they also store fat inside the abdominal cavity around essential organs. It is this fat that causes so many of the problems of being overweight. Not obese, just overweight.

It used to be thought that fat was just blubber, a fairly inert substance. This is now known to be quite false. Fat is a very active substance that produces a variety of chemicals. Abdominal cavity fat releases chemicals directly to the liver. If the effect on the liver is great enough, it causes a condition known as Metabolic Syndrome. This is indicated by two very easily measured data. The first is a waist measurement in excess of about 35 inches for men and 30 inches for women. The second is raised blood pressure. If you have these two indicators, you need to take action immediately.

BMI – Body Mass Index

This is a fairly crude index which compares your height and weight to give an indication of your weight compared to an 'ideal'. it is crude in that it takes no account of two very important factors.

The first factor is that your total weight depends upon the amount of muscle that you have as well as the amount of fat. Muscle is denser than fat. Therefore a very muscular person would have a high BMI indicating excess weight. A person with a very small amount of muscle would be indicated as having a smaller amount of fat than they actually have.

The second factor is as discussed above. It is not so much the total amount of fat in your body which indicates risk, it is where the fat is deposited.

Just in case you are mathematically inclined and interested in such things, the formula for BMI is:

(weight in kilogrammes) $\div$ (height in metres)^2

(weight in pounds x 705) $\div$ (height in inches)^2

BMI	indicates
< 18.5	underweight
18.5–24.9	normal weight
25–29.9	overweight
> 30	obese

Just to repeat, your waist measurement is a far more accurate predictor of dangerous levels of intra-abdominal fat than BMI. It also requires not much more than an honest look in the mirror and an accompanying reality check.

If you need to lose weight there are four things to remember:

- Eat less
- Eat the right things
- Lose weight slowly
- Exercise

Let's look at those one at a time.

Eat less

We Westerners consume HUGE amounts of meats

and other animal products which are not filling, and a relatively small proportion of the filling foods. The answer to that one is pretty obvious really; eat much less meat and eat more unrefined grains, vegetables and fruit. Your total calorie intake will be reduced and so will your intake of animal fats.

Eating quickly will inevitably lead to overeating and weight gain. Eating slowly will help to avoid these problems. The reason is simple enough. Your brain regulates your appetite by getting signals from your body. These signals take time. If you eat too quickly, the signals that indicate that you have eaten enough will arrive in your brain way after you have eaten enough. Therefore you will have eaten too much!

When your stomach is empty it produces a hormone called ghrelin. This sends a signal to your hypothalamus (a part of your limbic system) telling you to develop hunger symptoms. So you get hungry and start eating. The level of ghrelin falls slowly as your stomach gets filled, so the hunger symptoms also reduce.

As your small intestine begins to receive food, it starts to produce a hormone called PYY. This then sends a signal to your hypothalamus that you are becoming nourished and that it's time to stop eating. Again, this takes time to occur.

This is a typical balancing system with a time delay. It is rather like trying to control the flow of water through a long hose pipe using a tap. Turn the tap on, and the water takes time to get to the end of the pipe. Similarly, turning the water off doesn't stop the flow of water immediately. If you are filling a bucket with a hose pipe and turn off the water the moment the bucket is full, it will overflow because the water will continue to flow for a while. You need to stem the flow before the bucket is full if you want to avoid overfilling.

In order for this system of hunger hormone and fullness hormone to balance, you must eat slowly to give your body time to communicate with your brain when you have had enough.

Also, of course, when you eat slowly, you tend to chew your food more thoroughly which is a great aid to digestion and increases the enjoyment of food as you have much longer to savour the flavours in your mouth.

Your granny was right! You should chew every mouthful of food 48 times before swallowing. She didn't know exactly why you should do it, but now you do. Simple solution: avoid TV meals completely. Eat at the table and encourage family conversation.

Drinking water at meal times also helps reduce your food intake. The ancient yogic advice was that your stomach should be filled with one half food, one quarter water and one quarter air. The Islamic advice is one third each of food, water and air. Modern medics aren't as prescriptive, but the advice is to drink at least one glass of water or wine with each meal.

Eat the right things

You are what you eat. That's not quite right actually, but it's snappier than the correct version which is: you are what you consume and metabolize.

Our ancestors on the plains of Africa had a

tremendously varied diet of seasonal fruits, grains, pulses, berries and occasional meats. Once agriculture was developed and settlement became the norm, the diet became very much less varied, but still contained the essential elements for good health and growth.

Most of the staple elements of our diet fit into a fairly small number of food groups:

Whole-grain foods: brown bread, brown rice, oats, barley

Plant oils: olive oil, canola oil, soy oil, sunflower oil, peanut oil, walnut oil

Vegetables: leafy green vegetables, root vegetables

Fruit: apples, pears, bananas

Nuts/legumes: peanuts, peas, beans

Fish/poultry/eggs: oily sea fish, chicken, turkey, eggs

Dairy/calcium supplement: milk, cheese, yogurt

Red meat/butter: beef, lamb/mutton, ghee

Refined carbohydrates: white rice, white bread, white pasta, peeled potatoes

Plus *alcohol* in moderation

(The contents of each group is not exhaustive, but is simply intended to give a clear picture of the typical members. The list of food types is presented in a particular order. Those at the top of the list should form a larger proportion of your diet. Those lower down should be consumed in decreasing quantities.)

It is quite interesting to note that the foods higher up the list are precisely those which cause the greater release of hormone PYY – the 'fullness' hormone. The implication is obvious. If you need a quick snack to stave off pangs of hunger, a sweet or chocolate bar isn't the way to do it. There are many chew bars available these days containing grains and cereals which are much better. But remember that the hormones take time to be released!

A word on cooking styles is useful. Vegetables can be steamed! This is a much healthier way of cooking as the water soluble vitamins (the B group plus vitamins C and K) are then not leached from the vegetables. Microwave ovens are also excellent for cooking almost anything for the same reason.

Our modern diet frequently is under-varied despite the growth in world food trade. The foods we get are over-refined for the needs of shippers and storers rather than for nutritional needs. They are chemically enhanced to extend their shelf-life and to titillate the taste buds.

There is a great deal of conflicting advice about nutrition, particularly with regard to diets containing animal proteins, vegetarian diets and vegan diets. The jury is going to be out on this question for a long time yet. My own feeling (for what it is worth) is that our dentition, stomach flora, bile and vitamin needs indicate that we are omnivorous and that meat should therefore form a part of the diet. Despite all the lack of clarity on these issues, there is one consistent theme on which all dieticians of all inclinations are unanimous: eat fresh, eat unrefined, eat unadulterated with chemicals and eat variety.

Stress Busting

To put it as simply as possible:

- Eat fresh-picked fruit and vegetables rather than canned, freeze-dried or frozen.

- Avoid processed foods, particularly those with added salt and/or sugar (which is just about all processed foods!).

- Eat a healthy variety and proportion of foods from all the food groups.

- Reduce the amount of animal fats in your diet.

- Reduce the amount of refined sugars and carbohydrates in your diet.

- Eat more fish.

A very simple and powerful tool is a food pyramid. There used to be only the USDA food pyramid and accompanying booklet, but now there is a more up-to-date version created by Professor Walter Willett of Harvard University. These versions are different in the food groups they consider, but not hugely so. The greatest difference is that Professor Willett's pyramid is based on a regime of daily exercise and weight control. The one shown opposite is a greatly simplified version.

They both confirm the (essentially common-sense) advice given above.

If you design each meal to contain approximately the right proportions of each type of food AND vary the foods within each group day to day, your diet will be close to ideal.

This isn't as difficult as it might seem. A chicken salad sandwich on thick brown bread followed by an

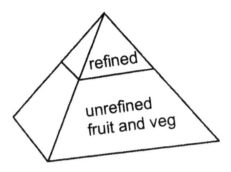

apple or banana and a small glass of milk is just about as balanced a lunch as you could wish for. A modern version of the traditional ploughman's lunch sold in many pubs is also pretty close provided that it is brown bread, the slab of cheese isn't too massive and the salad is a generous serving.

Interestingly enough, nearly all traditional diets fit the food pyramid very closely.

As an interesting aside, there is a great deal of anecdotal evidence that certain very common food additives can have extremely severe adverse effects on young people both in terms of their physical and intellectual development and their behaviour and attitude profiles. There is also anecdotal evidence from prisons that a diet based on pure, unadulterated foods leads to a reduction in destructive and negative behaviour patterns. This is an under-researched area but the indications are still pretty clear.

Don't forget the importance of drinking water regularly throughout the day. A dehydrated brain won't function properly, and a dehydrated body risks kidney stones and electrolyte imbalance.

Stress Busting

It is quite easy to determine whether your food and drink intake is healthy: you simply need to observe the waste products. Urine should be a pleasing 'light straw' colour. If it is too dark, you need to drink more. Your faeces should be firm, but not hard, and a fairly light brown colour. If they are hard, you need more fibre in your diet.

Lose weight slowly

Avoid all diets that promise fast results. There is no such thing as a fast and safe diet. If you try to lose weight too fast, you will actually gain weight! Again, this is because your body takes time to react to changes. This is another example of a balancing loop with a built-in time delay.

Actually, weight loss is a misleading term but it's one which is widely understood and I don't want to confuse the issue. It isn't weight loss that most people need, it's fat loss and muscle increase. Muscle weighs more than fat. For this reason it is impossible to suggest a rate of weight loss. At first you may well find that your weight increases if you add muscle bulk quickly.

For this reason, don't rely on the scales alone; they only tell you your weight, not the proportion of lean to fat. Your own awareness of your body is just as good a guide. If you start to feel and look better, you're on the right track. When you look and feel your best, you're there.

It's all down to our genes. We have evolved over the years to be resilient to times of famine. Those who best survive famine are those who are able to store the excess calories available in times of plenty in fat reserves. Then, in the famine, the fat reserves are called upon to provide energy. Those who didn't have the fat reserves disappeared from the gene pool. We are the progeny of those who survived. We are the ones who have the fat-storing genes. This served us well in the past, but it doesn't do so now. Our bodies are still programmed to store every available extra calorie as fat.

The speed of your metabolism depends on your body weight more strongly than anything else. (Blaming a slow metabolism for excess weight is a comforting thought, but it is a complete myth.) What happens is that when you reduce your calorific intake, your body thinks that famine is coming, and so reduces your metabolic rate to compensate. As your weight reduces, the metabolic rate falls at the same rate. You therefore have two factors serving to reduce the rate at which you consume energy.

If, when you reach your target weight, you return to old eating patterns, your new slower metabolism will be far more efficient at storing fat. Certainly, your metabolic rate will rise with your increasing weight, but there is a long time delay as you are still programmed to store fat.

You can see the pattern now, can't you?

You lose weight, and then gain more. Then you lose it again and put still more on.

But don't worry, all is not lost. This yo-yo effect, as it is inaccurately called, is not inevitable. What is needed is an awareness of how the system works and then to work with your system rather than against it.

Stress Busting

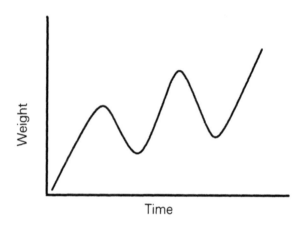

Time

You can use a three-pronged attack.

First of all, as mentioned above, your basal metabolic rate depends very strongly on your body weight, but there is another factor. Muscle burns more calories than fat. So if your body reduces the amount of fat and increases the amount of muscle at the same time, your metabolism will not slow down quite as much. Your weight control program needs to address the two issues of fat reduction and muscle bulk increase.

Second, you should reduce your calorie intake bit by bit in a planned manner. Certainly your body will react to your new reduced intake, but the reaction will not be as violent. It won't be a 'Hey, this is a serious famine coming' sort of reaction. Your metabolism will slow down more slowly and be much more closely aligned with your slowly reducing body weight.

Third, you need to increase your energy usage and hence increase your body's ability to convert fat into energy. You need more vitality. You need ...

Exercise

Warning: *Before you embark on any regime of unaccustomed physical exercise you should consult your physician. Failing to do so could have serious and possibly fatal consequences. Your doctor will be delighted to spend ten minutes giving you a clean bill of health. Doctors are doctors because they like doing that!*

Exercise is one of the best ways of reducing stress that there is. When you are deeply involved in physical or mental activity you cannot be stressed, so it is a wonderful and health-enhancing way of relaxing and unwinding.

Don't think exercise! Exercise has negative associations for many people. Instead, think ACTIVITY. This is also helpful when considering how you want to stay active. To get an idea of the types of activity that you need, simply think about our ancestors. What sort of activities did they have to carry out in order to survive? Your activities will need to have similar characteristics.

We can safely assume that the life roles of our ancestors were pretty different from ours. Skeletal and muscular differences indicate this quite clearly. Primitive societies still existing in parts of the world today are another source of evidence for this. Just think about the different physical activities they would have been carrying out and the physical abilities required for each one. Here's a brief analysis of some of the things a male hominid might have been doing as a part of his everyday life. You can look at the female for yourself.

Stress Busting

Hunting – stealth, grace, speed, strength, stamina, flexibility

Fishing – dexterity, hand/eye coordination

Gathering – stamina, eyesight, flexibility

Fighting – speed, reactions, strength, flexibility

Tool-making – hand/eye coordination, dexterity, patience

Mating – stamina, flexibility

Dancing – stamina, grace, flexibility, rhythm

If you look at the female, you will find different activities, but the same physical abilities.

Now, you are not a prehistoric hominid living on the plains of Africa, but, for optimum health, you still need the same physical abilities. If you lack any of them, you are going to be just as unsuited to survival in our modern society as your ancestors would have been in theirs.

There are three main aspects to optimum health and resilience to physical stress. They are:

- Muscular strength and endurance
- Aerobic fitness = stamina
- Flexibility and poise

Muscular strength and endurance

Your muscles are made up of two distinctly different types of fibre. They are called slow-twitch (Type I) and fast-twitch (Type II) fibres. The names explain pretty well what they do. The proportion of each that you have determines the properties of your muscles. A high proportion of slow-twitch fibres indicates a high degree of muscular strength. A high proportion of fast-twitch fibres indicates a greater degree of endurance. Not surprisingly, the type and amount of exercise that you do will determine the amount and proportion of each muscle fibre that you have in your muscles.

You don't need to build large muscles necessarily, but you do want your muscles to be firm. A famous heart surgeon was reputed to have said that before doing any surgery he always felt the patient's thigh. If it felt firm, he knew he was going to find a healthy heart to operate on. If it was flabby, he knew that the heart was going to be similarly flabby. This applies to both men and women.

Aerobic fitness

Aerobic fitness means having a strong and efficient heart and a good circulatory system able to carry sufficient nutrients and oxygen to muscles and essential organs. The only way to attain this is to exercise in the aerobic region for periods of not less than 20 minutes and not usually more than 60 minutes. Aerobic exercise means that your muscles are being worked at a rate which is high enough to require effort, but not so high that they cannot be re-supplied with fuels and oxygen by your cardio-vascular system. The stronger your heart and the

41

better your circulation, the greater your level of aerobic fitness.

There is a simple formula you can use to compute your ideal heart rate in the aerobic region. It is to calculate what is your maximum safe heart rate (= 220 — your age in years) and then to maintain between 60 per cent and 75 per cent of that rate. A whole industry has been built up around this formula. I strongly suggest that you ignore it completely. It takes no account whatsoever of your state of health in general or your vitality on any particular day.

A much easier and far more reliable way of doing it is simply either to talk to someone (or yourself) or whistle while exercising. As long as you are working sufficiently hard to raise your heart rate, but still have the wind for talking or whistling, you are in the right region. If you become short of breath, this is a clear indication that you have gone over the safe region and you need to slow down.

There are very many forms of aerobic activity, from brisk walking to organized aerobics classes. Choose one which you will enjoy.

Flexibility and poise

Having adequate flexibility will ensure that you do not suffer unduly from stiffness and joint problems. When you are flexible, your muscles are stretchy and able to allow the passage of blood more easily both to supply energy and to carry away the waste products. Flexibility also means strength, for weak and flabby muscles are not flexible. Having poise helps you move in an effective and efficient manner and maintain balance.

By far the best known and most popular form of flexibility training is yoga, which also helps develop poise through slow and graceful movement into and out of the poses. The old-fashioned primary school physical jerks of touch toes, side bends, etc. are almost as good and certainly more accessible.

The very best types of exercise are virtually cost free as long as you can resist the temptation to buy the latest in high-tech gadgets. You can, of course, go and buy a subscription to a health club. But be aware that most people pay their subscriptions and then don't use them. Now that is just asking for additional stress in your life!

Walking is by far the best all-round aerobic exercise. A brisk two or three mile walk every single day for the rest of your life will ensure that you remain strong and healthy well into old age. If you need proof of this, consider your friends who are keen walkers. You will see the benefits immediately.

The benefits of walking are numerous. Walking:

- develops both sides of your body equally

- massages your internal organs

- burns fat and not blood sugar (as long as you stick to the advice that follows)

- balances the brain, as both hemispheres of the cerebrum are used

- improves your poise and balance

- increases heart and lung capacity

Stress Busting

- gives you a chance to think and work out solutions to problems

- can be tuned to your energy level (high energy level – walk fast. Low energy level – walk not so fast)

- is just plain enjoyable

Please note that all this refers to walking, NOT shuffling.

You must start walking gently to begin with and gradually accelerate the pace over a period of five minutes or so. This is necessary to allow your body to realize that it is having demands made on it and to start to mobilize your glycogen and fat reserves into your blood stream. This is the warming-up period, ready for the fat-burning section of your walk.

The walking pace that you need to aim for is one where you are walking briskly but still with enough wind to hold a conversation. As long as you do this, you are maintaining yourself in the aerobic region and burning glycogen and fat in the muscles. You need to maintain this pace for at least 20 minutes.

Bring the pace back down again as you near the end of the walk to allow your muscles to clear any lactic acid (a by-product of muscular exertion). This is the cooling-down period and is essential to prevent excessive stiffness.

Imagine yourself to be the lord or lady of the manor making a tour of inspection of the grounds and take in your surroundings while walking with the grace and beauty that befits your (imaginary) status. Swing your arms naturally and think 'ANIMAL'.

There is really no better and enjoyable way of getting and staying in good shape than a daily brisk walk. You can also follow it with a bit of gentle bending and stretching to elongate the muscles again and encourage flexibility.

If you can get to a swimming pool easily, swimming is also an excellent all-round exercise. It involves working your muscles against a resistance and hence firms them up and also promotes cardio-vascular endurance. It is particularly good for those over a certain age with knee problems! It is ESSENTIAL to consult your doctor before taking up swimming if you are over 40. A heart attack in a swimming pool isn't funny for your family or particularly pleasant for the ones that have to fish you out!

Yoga and Pilates are both popular and wonderful ways of toning both the body and the mind. The body is toned by the poses, which can be quite rigorous and demanding at the higher levels. The mind is quieted by very deep concentration on the correct physical performance. Yoga can be learned from a book, but having a skilled and sympathetic teacher is a big advantage. Pilates really does need a teacher.

The martial arts are another all-round exercise. Many of these arts were developed to their present degree of perfection by professional soldiers. Their lives depended on the efficacy of their skills and on their degree of all-round physical fitness. These aspects are still taught, especially so in the more traditional of the arts.

The different arts all have different philosophies and bases. They may be 'hard' methods like karate, which is based on disabling blocks and devastating strikes and kicks. They may be 'soft' methods like aikido, which depends on redirecting offensive force.

Quite apart from the physical aspects of martial arts, they also teach discipline and mental agility. You have to be able to 'read' an opponent and react with appropriate speed, which requires very great mental focus.

Probably the most readily accessible art is t'ai chi ch'uan. In the beginning, the lessons revolve around a set of simple movements designed to promote strength, flexibility, poise, breathing and mental focus. At higher levels, some styles start to focus more on the martial aspects and introduce speed and agility.

Obviously, there are many games such as tennis, squash, football, hockey, etc. which all promote nearly every aspect of good all-round physical health. The choice is yours to make according to your own personality and needs. The only imperative is that you choose something.

Rest

You need somewhere between six and eight hours of sleep every day. If you don't get this you are very seriously damaging your entire organism. Your brain suffers as it doesn't get the opportunity to integrate and process the day's information. Your body suffers as it misses the opportunity to regenerate and relax.

Make sure that you get sufficient high-quality rest by designing and maintaining a sensible regime.

- Avoid drinking stimulants in the three hours before bed time.

- Avoid strenuous exercise in the two hours before bed time.

- Get into a restful mood before bed.

- Maybe have a shower or bath so you go to bed feeling relaxed and clean and comfortable.

- Keep the bedroom cooler than other rooms.

- Have the room as dark as possible.

- If you read to get to sleep, read as slowly as you can and choose non-exciting books. Your getting-to-sleep reading technique is exactly the opposite of your reading-to-learn reading technique.

- If you're a night owl, it's a good idea to set the alarm clock to remind you to prepare for getting to bed.

You CAN tune your body to get good rest no matter what your normal pattern has been in the past. It takes effort and discipline, but it can be done.

Deep muscular relaxation

It is vitally important for you to make the time for deep physical relaxation. The reason for this is simple enough: you cannot be relaxed and stressed at the same time. If you relax, you rid yourself of stress and give your system a chance to recover and repair itself.

There are two simple methods of relaxing your

body. Strangely very few people seem to be able to use both, but anybody can use one or the other. Experiment to find what works best for you.

For both methods you need to be seated very comfortably or lying supine on a comfortable bed. Both methods use Belly Breathing (as explained earlier).

If you are sitting, your head and shoulders should be above your hips, your spine curved naturally and your hands resting on your knees.

If you are lying supine, your spine should be straight and your neck raised slightly on a pillow and your head tilted slightly back (to fully open your windpipe).

Method 1 – All-at-once relaxation

This method is a way of relaxing your entire body all at the same time. The basic idea is that you will relax little, then a little more, and continue until you are in a state of complete relaxation.

1. Breathe in slowly through your nose for a count of 4, concentrating on your belly expanding.

2. Hold that breath without tensing your stomach muscles for the same count.

3. Exhale slowly and fully through your slightly parted lips for a count of up to 8. As you do so, feel your body becoming heavier and more relaxed.

The rhythm is:

In (nose), 2, 3, 4, Hold, 2, 3, 4, Out (mouth),
2, 3, 4, 5, 6, 7, 8

Continue for as long as you need until you are completely relaxed. The test for relaxation is simple enough – you cannot move without extreme effort.

Note: Concentrate your attention on your breathing, your posture and the feelings of deep relaxation. In particular, your posture must not become rounded or you compromise your ability to breathe into your belly and you will switch to Chest Breathing.

Method 2 – Progressive relaxation

In this method, you are going to take a tour of your body. You are going to start at your head, travel downward to your shoulders and arms and then continue down to your feet.
    The rhythm is identical to that above.

1. Breathe in through your nose as above.

2. Hold your breath as above and tighten the muscles of your face into a grimace. This will also tighten your neck muscles.

3. As you breathe out through your slightly parted lips, relax the grimace slowly until all the muscles of your face are completely relaxed.

Repeat, but tightening and then relaxing the muscles of the arms and shoulders.
    The order is then: belly, butt, legs and feet.

49

Stress Busting

If you wish, you can repeat the cycle in the same order (head to feet) or in reverse order (feet to head) until you are deeply relaxed.

You will find Yoga books that detail similar exercises, but with much finer groupings of muscles. There is little essential difference.

This method takes a little practice in order to isolate the different muscle groups, but works brilliantly once mastered.

Review

- Belly Breathing is a more relaxing and effective way of breathing.

- Eat a well-balanced diet comprising fresh foods. Avoid processed foods as much as possible.

- If you need to lose weight, do so slowly and according to a planned regime.

- Get plenty of fresh air and have an effective aerobic exercise regime.

- Get sufficient high-quality rest.

- You cannot be relaxed and stressed at the same time. Make time for deep physical relaxation.

4

Mental Resilience

- Introduction
- Creating a Calm Switch
- The sanctuary – real
- The sanctuary – imaginary
- Self-speak
- Music
- Mental imagery
- Meditation
- Journal keeping

Introduction

Your brain is an immensely powerful machine which is under your complete control. It often seems as though we are slaves to our thoughts, but in fact, the opposite is the case. By means of some simple and powerful techniques you can take control of your thoughts and the stress levels that you feel.

The set of techniques presented here is by no means exhaustive – you can find books which list dozens or more. Most of them are variations on a basic theme. What I have presented here are the basic themes.

Read all of the descriptions and choose those which you think will appeal to your particular personality or life-style. None of them will suit everybody, but there is nobody who cannot find something here of use. It is, of course, far better to be highly skilled in just one or two techniques that you can and do use effectively than to have a passing familiarity with a dozen or more that you can't or never use.

Creating a Calm Switch

One of the most valuable things that you can do for yourself is to create a Calm Switch. The technique relies on Neuro-Associative Programming, as developed by Tony Robbins. In this technique, you associate a simple action with a specific reaction or feeling. Once the association has been made sufficiently strongly, deliberately repeating the simple action is enough to generate the reaction or feeling that you want to re-create.

(Once you become skilled at this, you can invent exercises of your own to re-create any feeling you want at any time.)

Your Calm Switch is an association between touching the middle finger and thumb of your dominant hand together and a feeling of calm. Once the association is made, you can re-create the feeling of calm by deliberately touching your finger and thumb together. You will probably need about a week or so of practice to make the association strongly enough.

'One of the most valuable things that you can do for yourself is to create a Calm Switch'

Stress Busting

You need to set aside at least ten minutes of complete peace and quiet in a place where you feel safe from interruptions and disturbances and where there are no outside distractions. You also need to make sure that your clothing is non-restricting. Take off tight shoes and loosen belts and collars etc. Make sure that you are neither too warm nor too chilly. Everything must be just right for complete comfort and relaxation.

Before you start, it is a good idea to do some simple bending and stretching exercises to loosen up your body ready for complete relaxation. Some slow arm circling, chest stretching, forward, backward and side-to-side bending is quite sufficient. The idea is to get rid of as much physical tension as you can before you start, but you don't want to do too much or you will get your heart rate up. As long as you focus on releasing tension, you will do the right things to just the right degree.

Once you are physically limbered up, sit very comfortably in a chair. Place your butt well back as far as it will go, with your back well-supported, your feet flat on the floor and your shoulders comfortably at your side. Place your hands comfortably on your knees and do a few rounds of Belly Breathing with your eyes closed to relax yourself.

For this exercise, you are going to use Combination Breathing. This is breathing using your belly and your chest. First of all, you breathe into your belly and as your lungs become full, you expand your rib cage to fill them a little more. As you breathe out, your chest will fall and then your belly contract as you empty your lungs as much as possible.

Now touch the middle finger and thumb of your dominant hand together lightly and breathe very deliberately.

Each time you breathe in, feel the clean, fresh, life-sustaining air filling your lungs as much as possible, providing essential oxygen to your entire body and invigorating your brain. Feel the mental clarity that this gives you and notice how well you are able to concentrate on the physical sensation of breathing.

Each time you breathe out, repeat the word 'calm' to yourself as you press your finger and thumb together lightly. You will notice how you relax a little more with each outgoing breath as your lungs empty as completely as possible. Each time, you feel a little heavier and more relaxed.

After a few rounds, you may notice that you become very aware of your heart beating. That's good. You can use your heart as a metronome to count for how long you breathe in and out. You might also notice that you can hear all sorts of other noises going on inside your body.

Continue breathing and focusing on relaxation and calm for a few minutes. If you find that unwelcome and troubling thoughts come drifting into your mind, just allow them to drift out again. You can reject them by simply focusing your mind again on your breathing and any other body sounds you can hear. Don't become angry or frustrated, or the feeling of calm will evaporate.

When you are ready (and you'll know when this is) slowly prepare yourself to come back to full vitality and activity. Count down breaths from ten to zero and become ready bit by bit to be fully awake and raring to go when you reach zero.

You need to repeat this little exercise each and every day for at least one week. You will then associate the feeling of deep calm with the finger and thumb pressure. You can then generate calm at any time simply by performing this very unobtrusive action and repeating the word 'calm' to yourself, either under your breath or in your head.

Now, whenever you feel yourself becoming stressed or anger welling up, you can calm yourself down at will. I often go to the back of my classroom and do exactly this. It puts me in a good frame of mind to go round and do some monitoring and mentoring with the kids when they are busy on task.

The sanctuary – real

I have a special chair. It is directly in front of the stereo and I always keep that particular part of the room very neat and tidy. This chair is my sanctuary. I sometimes go there after the kids have gone to bed and when my wife is either out at one of her meetings or busy in another room. My sanctuary is a place of complete calm and peace and, like the sanctuaries of old, no one can come into my sanctuary and hurt me or disturb my peace and tranquillity. The right of sanctuary was abolished in England in 1723, but it still exists in my house!

You can create a sanctuary for yourself in your own house, or even in the car if you want to take a little drive out somewhere special. It's not so much the features of the place you choose that are so important, it's the feeling that you bring to it. Having said that, you do want the place to be one where you can relax and feel comfortable and unthreatened.

The sanctuaries of old were invariably places of religious worship and contemplation. This is exactly what you can use your sanctuary for. You may or may not feel the need for worship, but calm and quiet contemplation is a necessity, not a luxury. Visit your sanctuary whenever you find the need for some time when you can contemplate and consider things of greater or lesser importance without any outside disturbance. Here you can just sit and think and allow your mind to focus clearly on the things that concern you. Rather than just worrying about things, you can treat them to the full attention that they deserve. You will often find that a worry confronted is a worry defeated.

The sanctuary – imaginary

I also have an imaginary sanctuary, and this is quite some place. It is usually down a track in the jungle beside a small river in Casamance in southern Senegal (which just happens to be the most beautiful spot on earth), but sometimes (in the high summer) I transport it to a hillside just outside Lyons. It's simply too hot in this area of Senegal and the hillside just outside Lyons is always cooled by a gentle breeze.

I can't give exact details of my imaginary sanctuary. I redesign it and rebuild it very regularly to suit my particular needs at any time. It is always a short walk

Stress Busting

from where I have to park my (imaginary) huge American RV. It is painted white and has very heavy wooden doors. I approach my sanctuary on foot and always take very special care to drink in the beautiful surroundings. I listen out for the birds singing, look out for the insects and small mammals in the undergrowth and breathe in the scents of the trees and flowers. I want all my senses to be heightened by the time I enter my sanctuary.

More often than not it has five rooms surrounding a central courtyard. The rooms are: a kitchen, a shower room, a library, a gymnasium and a music room. I may decide at any time to change any of these rooms except the shower room. I do like to have a cooling shower and really close shave and then put on a nice clean robe and a pair of sandals.

After I have visited any of the rooms I require and fully prepared myself, I go into the courtyard. There, sitting at a low table, is my very own personal guru. I greet him and sit down with him. After some time we begin to talk.

He is a man of infinite wisdom able to listen to all my troubles and woes and answer any question that I may wish to put to him. He demands complete honesty from me and will listen to whatever I have to say without comment or passing any judgement. Occasionally, he will interrupt me and ask for clarification, but usually he just sits and listens. After I have said all that I want to say, he will answer any questions I want to put to him.

Because he listens carefully and has infinite understanding of all that I say and also of the things that I can't put into words but feel anyway, he can always offer the best answers. He has never yet let me down and I never expect him to.

Over the years he has helped me realize that I have to love my wife and kids for what they are, not for what I want them to be. He has also shown me that I frequently fall short of my own ideals precisely because I have set them high, and that there is no shame in that. He has reminded me of the wisdom of the ages and also introduced me to some new wisdoms. I have come to love this man and respect his every judgement.

My guru is, of course, me. My sanctuary exists solely as a place for me to consult my inner guru.

If you can create an imaginary sanctuary for yourself and take the time to consult your inner guru, you will find that the answers to all of life's questions are there within yourself.

Self-speak

Everybody speaks to themselves all the time, though many people deny it. You are constantly giving yourself feedback messages about everything that you do.

A few weeks ago I was visiting a school and was sitting in the staffroom waiting to see someone. In the adjoining workroom a teacher was sitting and muttering to himself quite clearly (I don't think he realized that I was there):

'Oh, you stupid fool. No, not like that. That's rubbish. Oh, for ****'s sake ...' and so it continued.

59

Stress Busting

When I went for my appointment I glanced over, expecting to see him marking books. In fact he was busy on his lesson preps and the fool he was speaking to was himself. I don't suppose for one moment that he would ever speak to another person in that way, but he was giving himself the most incredibly destructive messages non-stop.

Now, if you speak to someone like that, being negative and hypercritical and using quite strong language for 30 years or more, what sort of self-image will they develop?

In my research over the years I have found that this type of Self-speak is quite common. I've also found that it is destructive and reduces self-image and performance as well as leading to stress and a feeling of despair. Not only are the messages destructive, they are nearly always couched in the strongest of language which only serves to magnify the result.

What sort of messages do you give yourself? Try really listening to the way that you speak to yourself for a few days. You will probably be very surprised at the lack of respect you show yourself and at the overly-critical nature of the messages you send. These messages that you give yourself are very powerful and have a huge influence on the way that you perceive yourself. You should try to speak to yourself at least as kindly and positively as you would speak to anyone else.

It is natural to upbraid yourself from time to time, but take care to do it gently and use moderate language. Instead of telling yourself what a damned fool you are for driving too close to that taxi (or whatever), try being gentle and reminding yourself that you can drive better than that.

You can also create yourself a set of Self-speak cards and make a resolution to give yourself positive messages regularly during the day. These cards are 3 × 5 index cards or similar on which you write simple and positive messages. They must be simple because you are sending them to your other-than-conscious mind, and this level of consciousness can only accept simple messages. You can carry one or two cards around with you each day and keep on giving yourself these messages.

As an example, you might make a card which reads: 'Learn from your mistakes and do better next time.' Whenever you feel the need to upbraid yourself, take the card out and read it to yourself. Instead of calling yourself names, you can simply remind yourself that you CAN do better, but only if you learn from mistakes. If you simply swear at yourself, you will probably keep on making the same mistakes and continue giving yourself the same destructive messages.

Some people like to carry cards bearing quotations on them. There are thousands of sources for these words of wisdom, from the Bible to the Internet. For myself, I find Abraham Lincoln and Benjamin Franklin to be extremely rich sources, with Albert Einstein coming in a very close third. I particularly like them because the messages are simple and rely on plain statement of common sense. But, as we all know, common sense isn't actually that common!

Music

Different types of music evoke different emotions. Loud and raucous music stirs up loud and raucous behaviour; similarly, soft and gentle music soothes and calms. Recall how mothers sing to their babies. There are hundreds of different songs, but only a few different types. They are either play songs which are light and uplifting or lullabies which are gentle and soothing. Consider the different types of Christmas carols, from the uplifting 'Hark the Herald Angels Sing' to the almost hypnotic 'Away in a Manger'. The implication is obvious. If you want to relax and de-stress yourself, play soft and gentle music.

You can find very many tapes and CDs especially designed for relaxation. New Age music is usually restful and pleasant. Dolphin and whale calls, night-ingale songs, etc. set to music are also available. All of these are very effective and, played in the back-ground, create a calming and relaxing atmosphere in which you can get on with your life.

I have found that when my two boys come back from their karate classes their mental motors are fully wound up and running near the red line. Telling them 'Now, calm down, boys,' has no effect whatsoever. Playing relaxing music very gently in the background starting just before bedtime calms them down and prepares them for bed. I suspect that this is because it slowly brings down their brainwave frequencies from the high beta region to the lower alpha region.

For deliberate relaxation you need to get very comfortable and use your senses to get deeply involved with the music. Allow yourself to become totally immersed in the music and swept away. Move yourself gently to the rhythm (kinaesthesia) and try to get mental pictures (inner vision) of the moods that the music (audio) creates.

At the end of a busy and over-stimulating day, there is no better way of relaxing than having a pleasant drink while listening to calming music and allowing yourself to just drift on a cloud of contentment and peace until a deep sense of calm pervades your whole being.

My own favourite way of relaxing is to play a CD of African drum music I found in the market at £2.99. I close my eyes and follow the complex rhythms by drumming gently either on my thighs or very quietly on my bongos. Sometimes I follow the patterns exactly, at other times I pay a counter rhythm. I recall my days in Africa and conjure up the sights, sounds, smells and tastes of the markets. Within minutes I am transported to another level of consciousness and completely immersed. At the end of the CD I feel completely mentally refreshed and physically immobile.

In particular, listening to Mozart's music has been reported as being immensely stimulating of positive mental states. There is a phenomenon which has become known as the Mozart Effect. This is thought to be caused by the particular musical forms, frequency combinations, rhythms, etc. entraining brainwave frequencies and balancing the two hemispheres of the cerebrum. There is no absolute scientific proof as yet, but it's an interesting one to watch.

There is a growing body of anecdotal evidence that playing music in class has a similar calming and positive mental effect on difficult pupils. Music from the Baroque period is also an essential part of Accelerated Learning, so there might very well be something to it.

Mental imagery

Your brain doesn't know the difference between a happy situation and a happy mental image or a relaxing situation and a relaxing mental image. The result is that if you think happy thoughts, you will be happy and if you think relaxing thoughts, you will be relaxed. Thousands of reliable scientific experiments over the years have proven this to be exactly the case; you can literally think yourself into a happy and relaxed state. And remember, you cannot be relaxed and stressed at the same time.

Ever since ancient times storytellers have used their art to transport listeners to other places and times and fantastic situations. They have used a variety of techniques to do this, sometimes speaking slowly and quietly to indicate one situation and then speeding up and speaking loudly to indicate another. You can use exactly the same techniques with yourself to paint yourself a relaxing word picture to relax to. The technique is called guided imagery and requires the correct tone and speed of voice, and is helped by a relaxing musical background.

You have two choices. You can either tell yourself a pleasant and relaxing story in your head whilst listening to calming music or you can record a story for yourself over a musical background. For the latter, borrow the school's Coomber and use the CD player to play the music and a microphone to record the voice track onto the tape over the music. If your school is fortunate enough to have a proper audio lab, so much the better – you can use that.

No matter which route you take, you need to prepare yourself a script which you will find not only relaxing but also delightful. The more effort you put into the script, the better it will turn out. Most people like to create a script for a relaxing holiday in an exotic place miles away from anywhere. Don't worry if you've never been to such a place: it is exactly as you imagine it to be. Reality need not worry you at all. Incidentally, the cost of the flight is neither here nor there either.

Your script should describe the location in as much detail and involve your senses as much as possible. Don't just tell yourself that you're sitting on a beach: make it a clean, white, tropical beach with a clear blue sea lapping gently. Describe the view to either side and the sounds of the seagulls and the palms swaying gently in the cooling sea breeze and the buzz of the crickets as the sun starts to go down and turn the sky into a gorgeous crimson red.

The more overboard you go, the better it is. You want to transport yourself into the deepest sense of calm and sensual pleasure that you can possibly imagine. If you want to leave your spouse at home and bring in a nubile and scantily clad twenty-something to rub the jasmine-scented coconut oil into your bare upper thighs, that's OK too. A little eroticism never hurt anyone. It may not get your pulse rate down, but it's fun.

And you certainly won't feel stressed afterwards!

Meditation

All the previous mental relaxation techniques are designed to quieten and calm your mind basically by smothering unwanted thoughts with other, positive ones. Meditation, on the other hand, is a means of focusing the mind on a single entity and developing a profound understanding and oneness with it. The mind is allowed to wander where it will and simply observe the thoughts in a dispassionate and detached way.

Meditation is a very simple activity, but not easy. It takes time and a certain amount of discipline to get used to doing nothing. We Westerners are so used to being constantly busy that meditation can seem like a dreadful waste of time. It isn't, of course, but unless you try it, you'll never know that!

A famous guru was once asked by a reporter how long the average Westerner should meditate. The guru replied that twenty minutes was about right. He then quickly added that five minutes of meditation that you do is worth infinitely more than twenty minutes that you intend to do but never get around to doing.

There are three basic methods of meditation. All of them require that you sit very comfortably and breathe deeply and evenly (as for creating the Calm Switch).

Meditative breathing

Sit quietly and breathe easily counting the breaths as you take them. Count from one to ten, focusing your mind solely on the breathing. When you get to ten, start back at one again. As you breathe you will begin to notice other sounds as described before. Don't focus on them. As unwanted and distracting thoughts drift into your head, simply observe them and allow them to drift out again.

If you lose count and get distracted, don't worry about it. Simply re-focus your mind and start again at one. You are not in competition with anyone and you are not answerable to anyone. There is no blame and no compulsion to get it right all the time. There is simply you and your breathing. Nothing else matters for now and nothing else should concern you.

Mantra meditation

Choosing a mantra is often a problem for many people. 'What if my mantra doesn't work?' they ask themselves. It really isn't a problem. Simply choose another one. There is a degree of disagreement among meditators about the nature of the mantra. Some say that it should be a neutral word that doesn't conjure up any real meaning; it's just a means of maintaining focus. Others say that your mantra should have deep meaning and provide a basis for thoughts to drift into your head for you to observe. You can choose for yourself.

For myself, I usually choose a mantra which has meaning. I often use the word 'calm' and allow images and associations of calm to drift across my mind. On other occasions I'll use other words related to problems that I'm working on at a particular time.

Again, I observe the thoughts that cross my mind and allow those that seem fruitful to spawn other images related to them.

Contemplation

When you contemplate an object or text, you are allowing yourself to investigate it and allowing it to guide your mind in any direction. Two very common suggestions are a candle flame or an apple. Neither of these may seem very interesting at first sight. The whole point is that you are going beyond the first sight and investigating the meaning of these things much more fully. Again, you are simply a passive observer of the thoughts that the object or text evokes, but you grow in knowledge and wisdom as you observe.

The candle flame might lead you to think about where the wax came from. How does the wax travel up the wick? What really happens inside the flame as the liquid wax vaporizes and mixes with the air to burn and give off its light? Where does the light go to?

Even if you cannot answer any of these questions, or the many others that contemplation may generate, you will have benefited by knowing some of the many things that you don't know. And knowledge of your own ignorance is a vital step on the road to wisdom.

Of course, as our famous guru from a few paragraphs back indicated, even a short period of meditation has value. Just pausing for a moment or two to look at that apple in your hand and see the wonder of it is stress-relieving. Instead of just gobbling it up as you panic about those books that you haven't marked yet, allow it to speak to you quietly. It will tell you about the wonder of nature and how deep inside it lie the seeds that can create another tree for your children and their children to eat apples from. Puts those books into perspective, doesn't it?

Journal keeping

We are frequently assaulted with thoughts that can drive us to distraction. Keeping a journal is an excellent way of getting these things into perspective.

The problem with thoughts is that they fly in and fly out too fast for most of us to get a good grip on them. Writing things down forces a discipline of focusing the mind on problems and ideas in some detail.

There are two basic approaches to journal keeping, which you can mix and match as you like.

The first approach is to treat your journal as a place to simply record your personal history. This doesn't necessarily mean that it is a blow-by-blow account of your life. You can also include your thoughts and feelings and your dreams about the future. You might think of it as a history that your children may find after you are dead and gone and write it with them in mind. You may prefer that it is completely private and a place where you can write the very deepest secrets of your life without fear of being found out.

The second approach is to allow yourself to generate a stream of consciousness. You simply write and write and write without any thought of form or grammar, spelling or even coherence. After a while, you will find that your writing does become coherent and that things just pour out of you. They are quite likely to be things that you never even knew that you had inside in the first place.

In either case, using colour and shape in the form of concept showers or concept maps, highlights and maybe little cartoons will add to the pleasure and effectiveness of the experience.

Even as little as ten minutes writing your thoughts and insights on a regular basis will focus your mind on the truly important things and help you to put the trivial in its correct place.

Review

- You can easily create a Calm Switch to calm you down any time you want.

- You cannot be calm and stressed at the same time.

- Create a space and time for your very own private sanctuary – real or imaginary.

- Speak to yourself pleasantly. In particular, if you do 'tell yourself off,' do so gently.

- Listen, really listen hard, to relaxing music and allow yourself to drift.

- Go on an imaginary holiday whenever you need a break.

- Meditate.

- Journal keeping helps you see your life in perspective.

5

Emotional Resilience

- Introduction
- Proactivity
- Assertiveness
- Anger control
- Worry control

Introduction

In the previous two chapters I have used the word resilience without making any effort to define it. However, I feel that it is vital to define a precise meaning of emotional resilience as it isn't a concept which is met with too frequently nor which is immediately accessible. An understanding of the meaning is essential if this chapter is to have very much in the way of relevance.

Emotional resilience is the ability to thrive and remain emotionally stable in the face of adverse circumstances.

Please note that it isn't sufficient just to survive, we want to thrive. And there aren't too many jobs that present us with more adverse circumstances than teaching.

Stress Busting

That implies an ability to feel the stress but to bounce back; an ability to roll with the punches rather than to be floored and have to get up again. Just like a boxer, if you are floored a few times, it takes more and more effort to get up each time. Eventually you will be out for the count, have the fight stopped for you or have to throw in the towel. None of those three possible outcomes is acceptable. Defeat isn't an acceptable option.

That's quite enough of that particular metaphor. I don't really like to think of teaching as being a battle, but I have to admit that it does sometimes feel like one.

There are three strands central to having a high degree of emotional resilience. They are: (i) an openness about emotions; (ii) a high degree of self-control; and (iii) an ability to consider things objectively. What follows doesn't deal with these things explicitly, but they are implicit in every section.

Proactivity

I cannot do any better than to paraphrase the great Dr Stephen Covey.

> Between stimulus and response there is a space in which lies our freedom to choose our response, and that response determines our maturity and ultimate happiness.

The standard behaviourist idea is:

Stimulus → Response.

Dr Covey is stating that, for humans, the equation is:

Stimulus → [Ability to consider] → Response

We alone among all the creatures on the planet have the ability to choose our response to any given stimulus. And it is the response that we choose to make which determines how we are viewed by ourselves and other people, and the degree of happiness that we enjoy and that we convey to others.

The meaning of being proactive is that we take the time to consider exactly how we respond in any given situation, and do so in the most appropriate and constructive manner. The opposite is being reactive.

When we are reactive, we react to stimuli directly without taking the time to consider the appropriateness or otherwise. We thus cede control of ourselves to other people.

Proactivity is absolutely essential to your emotional resilience. If you are constantly reactive, you never have control over anything so you cannot possibly remain emotionally stable. If you allow others to determine your reactions, you will constantly be at the mercy of people whose agenda is very unlikely to be congruent with your own.

Being proactive is having a pause button and using it.

The pause button isn't a new idea by any means. We have always been told 'Count to ten' before responding. The advice is sound, but it's incomplete. What do you think while counting to ten? You have to use the pause button to give yourself time to generate an appropriate response: to think about how you will deal with this stimulus. The safest and simplest way I know is to ask yourself a little question:

'What do I want the outcome of this to be?'

You and the other person can either win or lose. It is axiomatic that the winner feels good about things and the loser feels bad. Being proactive means that you are looking for the best possible outcome. That can only mean that everyone feels good, so everyone needs to be a winner. There are only four permutations in any contentious situation. Your eventual outcome has got to be win-win.

Here's an example:

I had a very difficult situation with a Year 9 girl who simply could not enter my room without causing a riot. Once she was in the room, the riot constantly surrounding her continued. Because she was a very charismatic girl and one of nature's leaders, her raucous behaviour was incredibly infectious. She was quite incapable of realizing that her raucousness was the root of the problem – she thought that the entire world was raucous because the part of it surrounding her always was.

We sat down for a while (in detention) and talked about her feelings and mine. What sort of class she wanted and what sort of class I wanted. We discussed these issues at some length as I wanted her to realize that her behaviour not only prevented her own learning but also that of many other people. I gently explained to her that there were only these four possible outcomes:

I win, you lose. This means that I punish you and continue to do so until I have beaten you. If I cannot do this alone, I shall have to call in the bigger guns. Eventually, I shall emerge victorious and you will be humiliated and defeated.

You win, I lose. This is quite simply not an option. If I lose, the rest of the class loses. I will be unable to command any respect from the class and no learning will occur in my classroom. Eventually the entire school will be the loser because you will get the idea that you can win and rule the roost.

You lose, I lose. This is not an option. We shall both struggle to win and always be in conflict which will hurt both of us. It leads to an escalating spiral of punishment from me and unacceptable behaviour and resentment from you. This will only end with your suspension and probable exclusion. This will take some months during which twenty-seven of your classmates have their learning severely compromised.

You win, I win. In this case I get the quiet and diligent class that all of us want and need and you get the education that you tell me you want.

Now, what do we need to do in order to get to the win-win situation?

We agreed a system that would allow for her to enter the room early and to get settled down before the rest of the class entered. She committed to re-reading her notes from the previous lesson and keeping her head well down while everyone else was getting prepared.

She learned better (which is what she really wanted, but hadn't realized was possible) and I had the controlled and calm start to the lessons that I wanted. I won't pretend that all the problems were solved immediately. She needed the odd reminder, but that was easily accomplished. I simply needed to whisper to her from time to time, 'Win-win. Remember?' and that was sufficient.

We both won. That is proactivity.

Please note that there is absolutely no question of compromise here. In a compromise situation, both parties have to lose a little in order to gain less than what they actually want. In win-win, both parties agree to want the same things which are mutually beneficial. In all the textbooks on this you will find that the alternative to win-win is 'No deal'. This option doesn't exist in school. If a win-win situation is not possible, then it has to be win-lose in your favour. It has to be this way for the sake of the other kids.

Assertiveness

I was on the Tube in London one afternoon a few years ago. Beside me were two twenty-something girls. One said to the other that she had been on an assertiveness course the previous week. 'Oh,' said her friend, 'I've heard of that. What exactly is assertiveness?' 'Well, basically it's about bullying with such charm that no one realizes they're being bullied,' replied the first.

In order to dispel the many myths surrounding assertiveness, it's as well to define exactly what it is not and then see what we have got left. Being assertive is not about being:

- *aggressive* – using fear, threats and hostility

- *manipulative* – using emotional blackmail and guilt

- *offensive* – using personal attacks, name-calling and strong, overbearing language

- *passive* – not making waves and agreeing with anything in order to get a quiet life

- *passive/aggressive* – avoiding direct contact and working in the background to spread dirt and sabotage in order to get even

All these behaviours (which you will easily recognize in other people) are stressful both for the perpetrators and anyone else unfortunate enough to be on the receiving end. You will immediately see that they are self-defeating, frequently in the short term and always in the long term. You will also note that they are emotionally immature.

So, what is assertive behaviour?

Assertiveness is using effective communication to uphold your own rights and self-interest without trampling on the rights and self-interest of others.

The two most important watchwords are: respect and integrity. As long as you keep these in mind, you cannot go very far wrong. They are two simple enough words, but they have very many implications. Here's an exercise: make two concept maps, one for each word.

The benefits are:

- You get more of what you really want without rubbing others up the wrong way.

Stress Busting

- You get more respect, even from those who may disagree with you.

- You experience less soul-destroying frustration.

- You find fewer roadblocks due to interpersonal conflict.

This makes you feel better about yourself and improves your self-confidence. And it is true, justifiable self-confidence can only come from having an unshakeable belief that you are doing the right things in the right ways and for the right reasons. That is a vitally important idea. At least one wag has noted that the opposite of self-confidence is self-doubt and that self-doubt is almost like a living death.

Assertiveness is about effective communication, and communication is about the things that you say AND the way that you say them. It is about spoken language and body language. To communicate effectively you need to be, and be perceived as, a person with integrity, knowledge and a degree of passion.

In order to cut a huge topic down to size, it's a good idea to go back to the question that governs the whole of emotional resilience and then work forward from there: 'What do you want to outcome to be?' Once you have decided the answer to this, you will be in a better position to understand what, if any, changes you need to make to your behaviour in order to be assertive and hence more emotionally resilient.

You probably want to be proactive and a good team player and to encourage exactly those things in others that you deal with. So what do you need in order to achieve these things?

'To communicate effectively you need to be, and be perceived as, a person with integrity, knowledge and a degree of passion'

Effective body language

You only need to look around you at those who are effective communicators and those who aren't. You can always tell at first glance. Good communicators have poise and physical grace. Slovenliness and clumsiness are immediate killers of effective communication. If you want to be assertive you absolutely must stand or sit straight and as tall as you can and project yourself well. There is no mileage in being a shrinking violet.

You also need to be very aware of physical space and the way that you stand, and of correct use of eye contact. This is, of course, a cultural thing. There is no such thing as a universal notion of personal space. In the west, if you stand too close to a person and stare into their eyes too intensely, you will make them feel uncomfortable. If you stand too far away and avoid all eye contact, you will come across as being untrustworthy.

It is not possible to give any absolutes in this area. The only advice that I can possibly give is to be very sensitive to individuals with whom you are communicating. They will give you the feedback you need. Your job, then, is to be sufficiently relaxed and confident to be able to get your message across while being aware of the way the message is being received.

Effective spoken language

Consider again those people you know who are effective communicators. You will unfailingly notice that they don't 'Er ... um ... you know what I mean ...

like ...' and so on. They know exactly what it is that they want to say and they do so using, by and large, direct and personally relevant language. Any language teacher knows that spoken language is very different from written language. There are many false starts and incompleted sentences, etc. However, the train of meaning is always completed.

The very best advice here is, 'Engage brain before opening mouth.'

Effective communicators use language in a very skilled way.

They avoid imperatives ('You must ... should ... have to ...') and they avoid being mealy-mouthed ('It would be really nice if you could possibly see your way to ...'). Neither of these devices is likely to get you what you want.

Instead they tend to use one of two devices:

Statement/question

I'd like you to get your reports finished by Tuesday afternoon. Is that possible?

I need to have your stationery order by tonight. Are there any problems with that?

Your coursework plan needs to be handed in this time next week. Do you have any questions?

etc.

Using auxiliary verb <could>

Could you phone Mrs Smith at three-thirty?

Could you be at the meeting a little early, please?

Of course, tone of voice also has a great deal to do with your communication. Any one of the sentences above could be intoned in any one of several ways. A fairly flexible and genuine smile will always make the tone come out just right. On the other hand, a cold steely stare will guarantee that they sound aggressive and get precisely the result that you don't want.

These devices work very well when dealing with cooperative and reasonable people. Sadly, although such people form the huge majority of the population, there are times when we have to deal with those who are more easily described as difficult people. Some people are constantly difficult simply because (for whatever reason) that is the way they are. We should also recognize that anyone can be difficult at times of intense stress. (Yes, even you!)

There are many different types of difficult behaviour and each of them needs a slightly different approach. You will, however, notice that, in every single case, there is an underlying theme. The theme is that dignity and respect are maintained at all times. No matter what the stimulus, remember that you always have that little space in which to decide your response.

You also need to remember that very few people are difficult on purpose. If a person is presenting you with a conflict situation, it is likely that they simply don't have any other strategies for solving their deeply felt problems. If you rise to the bait of immature behaviour, there are only two possible outcomes. You will either win at their expense, or they will win at your expense.

There are three types of behaviour which we tend to see more often than most and where there is a distinct threat of dignity and respect flying out of the window. These represent a very real danger to teachers for whom these are very important things to maintain, so a brief analysis of them is very much in order. The types are given rather militaristic names. I'm not sure that I care for the metaphor, but it certainly does indicate that care is needed, and the imagery is sound.

Sherman tank: This person comes out with all guns firing and will run you over with no compunction whatsoever. They have a mission to fulfil and a war to win and nothing will stand in their way.

The best way to deal with the Sherman tank is to allow them to run out of steam. Allow them to rant for a while and only make neutral responses at first. You can certainly affirm their right to their feelings, but full agreement with them is likely to get you even more deeply embroiled. Telling them to calm down is likely to get exactly the opposite effect.

Once they have calmed down by themselves, try to get them to explain in neutral terms exactly what the problem is. Naturally, you discourage any abusive language and make it quite clear that you will not tolerate it. Ask open-ended questions to find out how they want to solve the problem.

'What exactly do you want me to do?' nearly always calms the situation down. Remember that anger is controlled by the lower parts of the brain. As soon as you ask for a considered response, you are asking for higher-order thinking. This is cerebral thinking and cannot take place when the brain stem and limbic system are in full flight.

If it is practicable, then agree a system for putting the solution into effect. If their solution isn't practicable, state clearly and calmly what can be done.

If your suggestions are met with resistance, the 'broken record' technique is useful. You simply repeat and repeat the same (perfectly reasonable) message over and over again until it is accepted.

Yes, Mrs Smith. I understand that your daughter likes to sit next to Cindy, but neither of them benefit from it.

Yes, I do appreciate that your daughter's feelings are important, but I feel that her educational progress is even more important at this stage. I am saying that they must sit apart in class for their own benefit.

You are, of course, quite right when you say that. But do you appreciate that their sitting next to each other prevents their learning anything? That is even more important. I insist that they should sit apart.

etc.

If it is rejected, help needs to be brought in.

Try to come to a clear agreement about what steps need to be taken to solve the problem and a clear statement of how you will both know that the problem has been solved.

Finish with an agreement that you will put your part of the bargain into effect and that you will either report back or wait for the other person to report back to you on their satisfaction or otherwise with the final outcome.

Sniper: This person will not attack you directly, but will hide behind a veneer of niceness and take pot shots from a safe distance. Snide comments and 'I was only joking' are unfailing indicators of this one.

Snipers need to be dealt with directly. A very clear statement of what is and isn't acceptable behaviour is needed. Make it clear to the sniper that there is no such thing as a safe distance from which to launch an attack, and similarly there is no safe armour to hide behind. When the inevitable 'I was only joking' comes, point out that it's only funny if everybody thinks it's funny. If one party (you) feels aggrieved, then it is just plain nastiness and you will not tolerate it.

Remember that you are being assertive and not rising to the sniper. You are not threatening any form of reprisal. Your language and demeanour have to be firm and simply show that you are fully in control of the situation and yourself. You are calmly stating what the laws of natural justice demand, and that you will not permit your rights to be trampled upon.

Landmine: This person is difficult to predict. They may explode at any moment if you touch the trigger. Of course, you don't always know where or what the trigger is.

Dealing with landmines is difficult, if only because they often take you by surprise with the violence of their reactions (which may be anything from sudden fury to floods of tears). The immediate (animal) response is one of the three fs – fight, flight or freeze. The only safe option here is freeze. Call an immediate time out. You need to give the landmine a chance to calm down and you need to avoid your own responses becoming inappropriate.

You will nearly always find that landmines are apologetic for outbursts. You can be supportive here and explain that you understand how stress can suddenly surface and that you appreciate the difficulties.

There are several other types of difficult behaviour ranging from the barrack-room lawyer to the wet blanket. These are all dealt with in slightly different ways. As long as you maintain an assertive outlook and remember the two watchwords, respect and integrity, you will have a very good basis upon which to build your assertiveness.

Unfortunately, from time to time you will find yourself in situations where others are being spoken about behind their backs. In order to maintain your own integrity and to send very strong signals, you should insist (assertively) that it stop at once and that you want no part of it. We all have opinions and it would be foolish to deny it, but voicing them in public to the detriment of others is not acceptable behaviour.

Anger control

Anger is a way of releasing a pent-up pressure. So is flatulence. Neither of them should be brought to public attention. Venting wind causes a moment's embarrassment. Venting anger risks losing respect and standing.

When anger meets anger it escalates out of all proportion and very unpleasant scenes can occur. You know perfectly well from experience that two angry people make a spectacle, completely fail to resolve anything, and neither brings any credit to himself.

When anger meets timidity the result is a completely false feeling of victory for the angry one and a feeling of humiliation and resentment in the timid one. Any witnesses feel nothing but distain for the attacker and sympathy for the attacked.

When anger meets assertiveness, the angry one looks like a fool and the assertive one gains a great deal of respect for expertly handling a fool.

Public displays of anger always make the perpe-trator look bad and are a sure sign of emotional immaturity. Grown-up and emotionally resilient people simply do not behave in that way. We don't tolerate children bullying other children and we must not tolerate anger being used to attempt to bully others, whether successfully or not.

Quite apart from the social unacceptability of anger, it has been shown by hundreds of studies to be extremely damaging to health. Those who get angry regularly or who carry their anger around with them for long periods are far more likely to die premature deaths than laid-back and easy-going characters.

Anger can be managed and drastically reduced by a couple of simple (and remember, that doesn't mean easy) strategies. Even if you do not feel yourself to be a particularly angry person, you can try these. Everyone benefits from at least thinking about these issues. You may well be able to help someone else who is not as calm and collected as they should be.

Keep an Anger Log

Simply make a note of the things that make you angry and the times when anger occurs. You will find that it is not situations that are to blame, but that your own feelings at the time had everything to do with it. This is a very valuable lesson to learn as it shows that you and you alone are the sole arbiter of your own feelings and reactions.

This may not be a very easy lesson to learn. The temptation is to say that a particular person, situation or thing makes you angry. It isn't quite as easy to say something like, 'My prejudices and opinions of < insert something here that riles you > combined with my general testiness make me angry,' even though it happens to be the truth. If it were not the truth, we would all suffer from road-rage, as none of us actually enjoys road hold-ups and inconsiderate driving.

Moderate your language

Instead of saying how furious you are with something or someone, say that you are a little peeved. Similarly, rather than venting your opinion that the Secretary of State is a stupid, uninformed and ludicrous hypocrite, you could just as easily think that (s)he could do with looking into the matter a little more deeply. Neither of these reactions will make any difference to the Secretary of State or anyone else for that matter, but there will be a world of difference inside you.

The language that you use when talking to yourself and other people says a very great deal about the way that you think. Never forget that the way that you think is completely under your control. It very often seems that thoughts have a mind of their own and just flow through us freely and of their own volition, but nothing could be further from the truth. Here's an exercise: Make a list of the words you habitually use when you are angry. Alongside, make a list of mild words you could replace them with.

Worry control

There can be no doubt that worry is by far the most corrosive and destructive enemy of emotional resilience. Whereas all the foregoing things we have discussed are transient phenomena, worry is an ever-present dysfunction eating away at the soul and causing raised levels of everything bad, without any saving graces whatsoever. If you are to be emotionally resilient, your absolutely must eliminate all worry from your life. It is destructive beyond belief.

As I mentioned before, your brain does not know the difference between real and imaginary happenings. The terrible things that you may worry about are just as stressful as if they actually happened. Given that people never worry about having too much fun or pleasure, it means that you are constantly living in a world of very real distress. It also means that your body and brain are constantly flooded with the chemicals associated with this state. As mentioned previously, you are not designed to live under these conditions and so you are causing immense damage to your entire organism.

Stress Busting

Now for goodness' sake, don't just start worrying about how much you worry and letting it prey on your mind that you are worrying yourself into a state of misery. You need to resolve to break the cycle of worry and eliminate it completely from your life.

Yes, that's right. I'm not saying that you should worry less. I'm saying don't worry at all. I'll repeat: resolve to completely eliminate all worry from your life.

What sort of things do you worry about? An upcoming Ofsted inspection? A particular child's behaviour? Maybe you worry about not meeting this or that target. Possibly you may worry that your budget isn't going to cover the new textbooks that the new syllabus demands that you get. I could cover several pages with worries that teachers have. And I suggest that you do exactly that.

Take a page in your notebook and write down all the things that you worry about. They can be the major worries that sometimes seem to fill your every waking moment: they may be the little niggling worries that just pop into your mind from time to time. They may be personal, professional, family, financial – in fact, all your worries. Don't leave anything out.

Once you look at them in the cold, clear light written there in front of you will see something amazing. Most of the things that you worry about you have absolutely no control over at all. You are worrying about things which if you worried about them non-stop from now until your dying day, they would not change one little bit. Other things that you worry about are things that you can control. They are probably the little niggles.

The answer is just so obvious, isn't it?

'Those things that you can deal with, deal with. Those things that you cannot possibly affect, forget about'

Stress Busting

Those things that you can deal with, deal with. Those things that you cannot possibly affect, forget about. The serenity prayer, made famous by Alcoholics Anonymous, puts it so well:

> Give me the serenity to accept the things I cannot change; the courage to change the things I can change and the wisdom to know the difference.

That's all very well, but how do you do it? Are there any practical steps you can take to put this undoubted wisdom into effect? As you might guess, I wouldn't ask the question unless the answer were an unequivocal 'Yes'.

There is a very simple idea that you can easily get hold of. There are two forces acting on your life: they are your concerns and your influence. Your concerns push you down and hold you back. Your influence lifts you up and pushes you forward. If your concerns are greater than your influences, you will always be subject to misery and stress. If your influence is greater than your concerns, you are able to make onward and upward progress toward the happiness and contentment that you really want.

Concern > Influence = ☹

Influence > Concern = ☺

You can probably see straight away that your concern is governed by your reactivity and that your influence is governed by your proactivity. You can also see that if your concern is greater than your influence, you are going to worry. If, on the other hand, your influence is greater than your concerns, you are empowered to deal with them.

You can completely eliminate worry from your life in a matter of minutes by taking two simple steps:

1. Identify the many concerns over which you have no control whatsoever and simply decide not to worry about them since it is pointless and destructive.

2. Identify the few concerns that you can reasonably control. Resolve to address them one by one until they are no longer negative pressures in your life.

This means that you are in control, which is a primary tool in reducing your stress.

Review

♦ Proactivity means that you decide for yourself what your response is to any stimulus rather than allowing others to control you.

♦ Assertiveness means that you stand up for your rights without trampling on the rights of others.

♦ Realize that your anger is caused by your reaction to events, not to the events themselves.

♦ Worry is completely pointless and incredibly destructive. Don't worry about anything. If it's out of your control, accept it. If it's in your control, change it. Know the difference.

6

Quick Tips

Design your day

All the stuff in the previous five chapters is all well and good, but if you don't do any of it you will simply be well-informed and still stressed. Changing the way you feel means changing the way you do things, just because the way you do things makes you feel the way you feel.

Design your perfect day with islands of calm at regular intervals. This has to be a deliberate effort. It certainly won't happen by accident.

Make sure that you start the day well. Have a good, nourishing breakfast and leave home in good time so that you don't arrive at school late and in a frazzle.

ALWAYS make time for a proper lunch break. You will work much more effectively and efficiently in the afternoon for allowing yourself at the very least twenty minutes to sit down calmly and eat a light lunch and maybe have a chat or read something easy.

If you stay late, have a short break at the end of school before starting on your admin. and other tasks. Again, you will get them done much faster for recharging your batteries for a few minutes. Remember that there is a big difference between being busy and being productive.

Make sure that your homecoming is a joyful occasion. If you are the first home, make sure that you are ready to greet the rest of the family in a warm and happy frame of mind. If you get home after others, greet them warmly and re-involve yourself immediately. After all, the family is probably one of the main reasons for having the job in the first place (very few people have a family in order to support their job).

Make very sure that you allow at least thirty minutes every evening for physically tiring exercise.

Also allow at least the same time for real meaningful communication with everyone in the family. By the way, gawping at the same nonsense on the same TV in the same room doesn't really count as quality time.

Have a bedtime ritual. It takes about twenty minutes for your brain to slow down from the everyday state to the sleep state. People who say they are asleep the moment their heads hit the pillow are already well relaxed when they get to bed. If you aren't, you are inviting sleep problems.

Design your school days

Mat Jarvis is one of the leading experts in teacher stress. He is very much of the opinion that efficacy and stress are in inverse proportion. Highly efficacious teachers are lower stressed than their less efficacious comrades.

Efficacy is a nice word. The dictionary definition is that it means more or less the same as effectiveness. However, in Stress Management and Time Management circles it means effectiveness AND efficiency.

Stress Busting

An effective teacher is one who gets the job done. An efficient teacher is one who gets the job done in a reasonable time. You need to consider both effectiveness and efficiency. The more effective you are, the more reward you get from the job and the less likely you are to resent the unreasonable demands made on you. The more efficient you are, the less time you need to spend in pointless busy-ness and you spend more time on achieving the results that really matter – helping the youngsters a little way along the never-ending road to becoming lifelong efficacious learners.

Being efficacious requires a certain mind-set:

1. Think about what you are going to do.

2. Do it.

3. Think about what you did so you can do it better and faster next time.

If I were asked to summarize both Stress Management and Time Management into a single sentence it would be: 'Separate your thinking and your doing.'

If you learn only one thing from this book, it should be that single sentence.

Design your exercise/activity regime

Do you remember that stuff about fast-twitch and slow-twitch muscle fibres? For optimum health you need activities that both build or maintain a good muscle bulk and promote muscle endurance. You won't find a regime that does both these things by accident.

The only single activities that do both these things in reasonable proportion are the martial arts and higher levels of yoga and Pilates.

Muscle bulk building/maintaining needs appropriate training three times a week and no more. You need the rest days for the muscle fibres to repair themselves. Endurance activities should be done at least four times a week.

Hey! You've got an activity a night. All you need to do is to choose and timetable. Excellent health is yours well into old age!

Feed your body/brain

It's a very good idea to create a basic family or individual menu. It doesn't need to be anything like, 'It's Tuesday so it's hotpot,' it's just there to ensure that your daily and long-term nutritional needs are met. In particular, most dieticians recommend that you should consume at least two portions of oily fish per week. This is to ensure that you get sufficient omega-3 fatty acids which are essential for adequate production of myelin to protect and nourish neurons.

You don't necessarily have to beat yourself up making sure that every single meal is balanced according to the food pyramid, but you should ensure that every day provides an adequate intake of all the food groups.

The jury is still out on several important issues (for example, is it better to graze or feast and fast?) and probably will be for a long time, but balance is never going to be off the menu. And your own body will tell you most of the answers as long as you are sufficiently sensitive to attune yourself to it.

Feed your mind

Read good books. It doesn't really matter what you think of as being good. There is no room for snobbery here. Reading is de-stressing and a wonderful way of spending your time.

Fancy going for a higher degree? Do you realize that if you spent 30 minutes in focused reading every school day evening for a year you would have completed 100 hours of reading? Do that for two years and you have done all the required reading before you even start your course. And just think of the garbage you will have missed on TV.

Wherever you are, be there

I cannot think of anything more ridiculous, and I do it myself, so I won't be too critical. But I still advise it anyway.

Don't take home problems to school. When you are at school, be at school. Be in every sense of the word.

Don't take school problems home. When you are at home, be at home. Be in every sense of the word.

As one wag put it: be a human being, not just a human doing.

Plan for success

If you want to advance your career, plan it. Decide what extra qualifications and experience you need and write yourself a road map. Your SMT will be absolutely delighted to help you out on this. They have all been through this process themselves (if they hadn't they wouldn't be SMT), and can point out everything that you need to know. They will confirm that no one ever reached a senior position by accident.

Dress for success

You will always look better and feel better if you wear good clothes well. You will also be treated better by kids and colleagues alike. Have you ever seen a scruffy head teacher?

Stress for success

Remember the performance-stress curve! You do need a certain amount of eustress in your life. Without it life is going to be boring and uninteresting. Set yourself targets, reachable targets but not too easy, and go for them. You do need a bit of 'oomph' in your life.

Recommended Reading

Butler, Gillian and Hope, Tony (1995) *Manage Your Mind*, Oxford Paperbacks.

Buzan, Tony (2001) *Head Strong*, HarperCollins.

Carnegie, Dale (1990) *How to Stop Worrying and Start Living*, Vermilion.

Carnegie, Dale (1994) *How to Win Friends and Influence People*, Hutchinson.

Covey, Stephen R. (1999) *7 Habits of Highly Effective People*, Simon & Schuster.

Davidson, Jeff (1997) *The Complete Idiot's Guide to Assertiveness*, Alpha Books.

Elkin, Allen (1999) *Stress Management for Dummies*, John Wiley.

Helmstetter, Shad (1991) *What to Say When You Talk to Yourself*, DK Publishing, HarperCollins.

Henderson, Roger (1999) *Stress Beaters*, Metro Publishing.

Mulligan, Eileen (2001) *Life Coaching for Work*, Piatkus Books.

Robbins, Anthony (2001) *Awaken the Giant Within*, Pocket Books.

Wetmore, Donald (2001) *K. I. S. S. Guide to Organizing Your Life*, Dorling Kindersley.

In addition, I would strongly recommend anything written by Tony Buzan, Stephen Covey, Tony Robbins or Dale Carnegie.